Rainbows Through The Storm

Facing Tragedy, Finding Faith

Holly Campbell

God Bless!
Holly

INTHEDEN
GRAPHICS

Scripture taken from the HOLY BIBLE, NEW INTERNATIONAL VERSION. Copyright © 1973, 1978, 1984 International Bible Society. Used by permission of Zondervan Bible Publishers.

Edited by Ron Carr

Cover artwork by Carol Ellis

Cover design by Nathan Parson

Printed in the United States of America

ISBN-13: 978-0-9776136-0-1
ISBN-10: 0-9776136-0-7

This book is dedicated to my children: Sarah, Dustin, and Stephen Campbell. Two are in Heaven and one is here on Earth providing love and joy and giving us hope for the future.

Sarah Danelle Campbell
(December 2, 1979 – June 14, 2000)

Dustin Lee Campbell
(February 25, 1983 – September 29, 2001)

Stephen Dale Campbell was born August 30, 1988, and is my reason to continue. Thank you Stephen for being my son and supporting me.

Contents

Letter to God

April 3, 2004

Dear God,

I don't understand. Why did You let my children die? Did You think they would be better off in Heaven than here with me? Wasn't I doing a good job? Was it because of sin in my life? I wish I knew the answers. I try to have faith. I know You are taking better care of them than I did, but I miss them and I feel like I need them more than You do. Their deaths affect everything I do and I never stop thinking about them.

Philippians 4:13 says, "I can do all things through Christ which strengtheneth me." I know I wouldn't survive if I didn't believe in You, so I cling to special Bible verses like this one. Another is Psalm 46:10, "Be still, and know that I am God." I began quoting that one to myself when Sarah died and it has helped me. Still, it is so hard to understand.

When I start believing Satan's lies I get frustrated and angry with You, with myself, and everyone around me. It's not fair that Stephen has to grow up without a sister or brother. But God, with Your help we will survive.

My friend Tom has asked me to think about writing a book to help others. I am willing to try. But Lord, I will need Your help because I don't want this to be just another book about grief with shallow advice and pat answers. I want Sarah's and Dustin's life to be used, not wasted. I want this to give hope to someone who is going through tough times. Lord, I am committing this book to You and I need Your love and grace. So, here goes.

Love,
Holly

Introduction
by Dr. Tom Fuller

I met Holly Campbell in a cemetery on a gray, overcast day in the Texas Panhandle after a funeral I had preached for a young man who took his own life. Holly and her husband Danny stood in support near the grieving family. Afterwards, Holly stepped up, introduced herself, and later led me across the cemetery where she showed me the graves of her daughter Sarah and her son Dustin.

Despite their double tragedy, the Campbell's attitude was courageous, positive, even heroic, in my estimation. Since then, Holly and I have carried on many conversations about death, repeatedly returning to questions so many have asked down through the centuries: Why does God let good Christian families suffer great loss? If the Holy Spirit is our helper and protector, why did He not help and protect Sarah and Dustin? Even before their births, Holly and Danny had asked the Lord to protect their children from harm. Did God ignore those prayers? Does praying for our families do any good? If God had our kids in His mind from the foundations of time, why does He allow their seemingly senseless deaths before they can fulfill His purposes? If God is omniscient (all-knowing) and omnipotent (all-powerful), couldn't He have stepped in and prevented their deaths if He had wanted to? Why do self-centered, destructive, purposeless people live on and on while the good die young? The bewildered author of the Old Testament book of Ecclesiastes wrote: "In this meaningless life of mine I have seen both of these: a righteous man perishing in his righteousness, and a wicked man living long in his wickedness" Ecclesiastes 7:15 NIV. Yes, we have seen that happen also and we have wondered, "Lord, why?"

I was so impressed with Holly and Danny's noble and honest way of facing their tragedy that I invited them to come to the Methodist church where I served as pastor to speak one Sunday morning. Together they stood in the pulpit and told their story. Before they had finished, the sanctuary was awash in tears. We parents realized we could have been the ones standing up there. Only by chance…or something… were our kids spared.

I encouraged Holly to write a book that she might share her journey with others. She agreed, though reluctantly, for she does not consider herself an author. Nevertheless, she would record her experience, her honest feelings and thoughts, not merely those that good Christians are supposed to have. Then she would give insights into what has helped her and her family keep their faith in God and continue on with life.

Chapter 1
Our Family

I was born in the small Texas Panhandle town of Friona on June 6, 1957. I have lived here all my life except for the time I was in college at West Texas State University in Canyon, located near Amarillo. I grew up in a loving Christian home with my wonderful parents, Dale and Laura Hart, and two sisters, Karene and Evelyn.

When I was a college freshman my baby brother Jeremy was born. My paternal grandparents lived next door and played an important role in my early life. My other grandparents also lived in Friona. I have always been blessed to have family nearby.

We raised shorthorn cattle and sheep in our local 4-H program and I won many 4-H awards at livestock shows during those years.

We attend First Baptist Church in Friona and I gave my life to Christ when I was a senior in high school. I married Danny, my high school sweetheart, in July 1977, two years after graduation. A few years later we began our family: first Sarah, then Dustin, and finally Stephen.

Danny is an electrician and I am a real estate broker. We are both self-employed. We live next door to my parents and across the road from the house where I grew up. You can assume I have lived a sheltered life! I enjoy taking photographs, riding my bike, exercising, snow skiing, going to the mountains, camping, and going to the lake.

Chapter 2
Our Children

Sarah was our first child and only daughter. From the day she was born she had her daddy wrapped around her little finger. As she was growing up, before she discovered boys and cars, Sarah was his favorite fishing buddy.

She enjoyed the same things her dad did and their outlooks on life were pretty much the same. She was a joy with lots of energy, talent, and beauty. Strong-willed and independent, she accomplished everything she set out to do.

As a baby and a young child Sarah did things her way. As long as she had her pink baby doll and her blanket she was happy! We never knew what she was going to do or say and she kept everyone around her entertained throughout her short life.

When Sarah was three years old her baby brother Dustin entered our family and he instantly won my heart. He was a momma's boy all his life. He became Sarah's best friend early in life. They were always close and had so many fun times together.

Sarah started kindergarten and decided that Dustin also needed to start learning. So, at the age of two, Dustin could recite the "Pledge of Allegiance" perfectly because he wasn't

Stephen, Sarah, and Dustin when Sarah came home from
college on her 19th birthday in December 1998.

about to disobey his very strict teacher and big sister.

Dustin was easygoing and lovable. He sucked his thumb and carried around his baby blanket until he started kindergarten. The day he turned five years old he quit sucking his thumb and started growing up. Dustin was the entertainer in our family. He could imitate almost anyone's voice and kept everyone around him laughing most of the time. He was a good athlete and had the self-confidence to do anything he wanted. He had a cute little grin that everyone who knew him loved!

We were blessed with one more addition to our family when Sarah was nine and Dustin was five. I had a name picked out for our new baby, but Sarah was so disappointed she didn't get a baby sister that we let her name her little brother. She named him Stephen, and his middle name is Dale, after my dad.

Sarah and Dustin adored Stephen and he followed them around everywhere they went, including all the tennis, track, basketball, baseball, and football games in which they participated. Sarah was a wonderful babysitter. She would spend hours pushing Stephen around in her doll buggy and little red wagon. Stephen's personality is a mixture of Sarah and Dustin. He is smart and funny with a dry sense of humor. As a teenager, he suffered more tragedy than most people do in a lifetime. However, he never used their deaths as a crutch.

Like Dustin, Stephen is strong and athletic. He played football, baseball, and threw the discus in track. We have fun playing ping-pong, and sometimes I can actually beat him! Stephen loves to fish almost as much as his dad does and they enjoy fishing in tournaments together.

Stephen keeps me going. He is fun and a joy to be around. I cherish our time together.

Chapter 3
Sarah

Sarah loved challenges and quickly became bored with endeavors that did not challenge her mentally or physically. She excelled in tennis, piano, and flute. She took woodworking and built a beautiful grandfather clock and cedar chest which won awards at state competitions. When Sarah was a high school senior she went to our credit union, borrowed money, and began taking flying lessons in Clovis, New Mexico.

She graduated from high school in May 1998. Two days before going to college at Southwest Texas State University in San Marcos, Texas, she received her private pilot's license. What an exciting day that was!

Sarah was ready for her new life. It was really hard watching her drive away in her little green Pontiac Sunfire knowing she would be 500 miles away. Of course we followed her to San Marcos but knew that for the first time we would be coming home without her.

She came home from college at Thanksgiving. We went to the Clovis airport and she took me flying on Thanksgiving Day. What a special and fun memory I have of that day!

Sarah came home after her first semester and told us she

Clockwise from top left: Sarah's senior picture; senior prom;
high school tennis; and off to college.

didn't want to go back to college, but wanted to continue to live in San Marcos. After explaining to her that we would not support her financially if she didn't go to classes she said, "That's okay. I already have a job at the San Marcos airport." Sarah was very independent and soon proved to us that she could make it on her own.

She worked at the airport and flew every time she could save the $60 cost per hour to fly. She lived there almost two years.

Sarah was a loving, forgiving person. She was never prejudiced against anyone and accepted people for who they were. The high school counselor told us that Sarah was one of the smartest and most talented students she has ever seen. She was creative and I don't think her mind was ever still for a second.

She bored easily and I believe this accounted for the times she got into trouble. She was completely honest, even if that meant hurting someone's feelings. I always loved for her to help me clean out my closet because she didn't mind telling me if something was ugly or didn't look good on me. On the other hand, she would tell me if I looked pretty or if she liked something. She was that way with everyone she knew. Her friends have said that Sarah was the most real person they have ever known.

On June 4, 2000, Dustin and I drove to San Marcos to be with Sarah for a routine day surgery to remove cysts

Top: The day Sarah received her pilot's license.
Below: Sarah and I in San Marcos the morning of her surgery.

from her ovary. We went a day early so I could celebrate my birthday with Sarah and Dustin.

Her surgery was on June 5th, and it was more complicated than expected so the doctor admitted her to the hospital for the night. The next day we took her back to her apartment. The pain did not go away. Sarah wanted to come home with us so we got permission and brought her back to Friona to recuperate. She was so happy to be home. She enjoyed lying on the trampoline and looking at the stars and the sunsets, but she especially loved being around her two brothers.

We stayed in daily contact with Sarah's doctor and he believed everything was normal. By Sunday, June 11th, the pain worsened and we knew something was seriously wrong. We took her to our local hospital. After some blood work they sent us to a surgeon in Hereford, Texas, a larger town nearby.

Around midnight Sarah underwent emergency surgery. The surgeon removed her ovary and thought her medical problem was solved. The next day Sarah felt better. She got out of bed and walked around a little. We were beginning to feel encouraged. Her doctor was still concerned because her platelet level was low despite the blood they had given her. Danny spent the night at the hospital with her and the next morning she seemed much improved.

On Tuesday morning the surgeon told us he wanted to

transfer her to Amarillo to see a hematologist because her platelets were still too low. Seconds after I left her room to prepare for the trip Sarah had a sudden seizure and lapsed into a coma. She was rushed by helicopter to Baptist St. Anthony's Hospital.

In spite of seven doctors treating her, she continued to worsen. Her liver was destroying her platelets faster than the doctors could give her blood. To further complicate matters, her kidneys had stopped working. The team performed another emergency surgery in an attempt to stop the hemorrhaging.

By this time many of our family and friends were with us and prayer chains had been started by different churches.

Literally thousands of people were praying for Sarah, some as far away as Australia. Intensive care unit nurses and staff family advocates as well as many others at the hospital showed us tremendous kindness. I promised God that if He let her live I would be a better wife and mom. Whatever He wanted me to do I would obey if I could just have my daughter back.

Since Sarah was a runner and tennis player, her heart was so strong it continued beating several hours longer than it should have. Danny and I held her and watched helplessly as she slowly bled to death. We felt confused and angry. We had trusted God. We knew and believed He would heal her.

At 8:15 p.m., June 14, 2000, Sarah's breathing stopped

and the doctor was called. We held each other and cried, then drove home in shock not knowing what to do next.

When we arrived home we discovered our friends had cleaned our house, done our laundry, and mowed the yard. I couldn't understand how they knew she was going to die and I didn't. The next few days and weeks were a blur.

Hundreds of people attended Sarah's funeral. Her cousin Lissa Bass created a music CD. She and some of Sarah's high school friends helped us plan the service. Sarah's friends; Tiffany, J.T., Cate, and Renee came from San Marcos and were here along with many childhood friends. Our friend and former pastor Waide Messer drove to Friona to speak at her service. Our funeral director John Blackwell came to our home, gathered pictures, and presented a video about Sarah's life.

My friend Patsy Allen made a bookmark to hand out to everyone. It was a picture of Sarah and her airplane with a note written by her dad. Carnations were given to all the young people who attended. It was really amazing to watch how everyone took over for us.

Three days later we had to make the drive to San Marcos to clean out Sarah's apartment and bring her car home. We went through the motions and somehow did what had to be done. Her college friends were there to help and support us.

I felt helpless and confused. I couldn't believe this was happening. It was almost like it was happening to someone

Sarah

Thank you for the dance we shared. You are leaving more than just an enormous hole in our life. You have shown us how to love and forgive like no one else. The Lord blessed us with you for twenty years and the pain we have now is a small price to pay. We now know how fragile life is and how important it is to say "I love you". You will be in our hearts forever.

The bookmark handed out at Sarah's funeral.

else. I felt like I was in a horrible nightmare and couldn't get out. Sarah was so full of life that it wouldn't sink in she was gone.

Everywhere I looked I could see where she had been and things she had done. There were still cupcakes in her kitchen that she had made me for my birthday. Nothing was making any sense to me at this point and I was about to discover feelings, hurts, and loneliness unlike anything I had ever felt in my life. We tried to cope with our feelings by staying as busy as we could.

A couple of weeks after we got back from San Marcos we had a truckload of rocks delivered to our home. Danny, Dustin, Stephen, and I began building a rock garden and when it was finished we planted flowers from the funeral. Some of the kids' friends and several family members also came and helped. Before long it was a beautiful place that we still enjoy today.

Dustin and Stephen designed the walkway out of flagstone. Our friend Jackie Stowers made me an airplane that we have beside the garden. I've often used the garden as a background for photographs.

The rock garden at our house. We planted flowers from Sarah's
funeral and the airplane was built by a friend in her memory.

Chapter 4
Dustin

Sarah's death affected her brother Dustin more than anyone else. They were best friends. Even though Sarah was three years older and away at college they stayed in daily contact and shared their secrets and dreams. They often stayed in trouble because of the large long-distance bills we received each month. After Sarah's death Dustin held his pain inside so we couldn't see how much he was hurting and struggling for ways to channel his grief.

Dustin was beginning his senior year in high school. His little brother Stephen was entering the sixth grade. We were all searching for a much needed distraction from the hurt we were experiencing.

With school in full swing we focused on Dustin's football and other senior activities. Dustin was strong and athletic. He was named All-District defensive end in football but when the season ended he was still lost. He fell away from God and seemed to drift.

In Dustin's English class his senior year, he had to write a paper about his hero. Here's what he wrote:

Clockwise from top: We gave Dustin a yellow Jeep for high school graduation; his senior picture; and a playful time with his dog Buddy.

"My Hero"

"Over the years I have accumulated many different role models and heroes. One person in my life however has touched me more than anyone; my best friend, my sister, and my hero, Sarah Campbell.

Since Sarah and I were little kids, we always had a special bond, more than most brothers and sisters do. Being three years older, she taught me very much about life and about people. My sister was a very outgoing person who would always stand up for what she believed. She always thought about others first, which always managed to make friends, and keep a good job.

Sarah played tennis and loved it during all four years of her high school career. During her senior year she took flight lessons in Clovis. Flying was her love. She always felt so free from the world when she flew. She worked very hard to pay for her lessons herself. Finally after graduation, she got her private pilot's license, which she was very proud of.

Sarah lived in Friona for all of her school years, which she hated every minute of. She knew there was a big city with more opportunity out there just waiting for her. After graduation she packed up her things, said goodbye to her friends and family, and headed to San Marcos, Texas. She attended Southwest Texas University and worked at the San Marcos Airport. We kept in close contact and I visited her periodically. She was still always there for me when I had a problem or needed advice.

On my last visit to see her, my mother and I took her to the hospital where she was supposed to have "day surgery" for internal pains, and go home the same day. After surgery, she felt terrible, as did she the second day. We talked her into coming back to Friona until she felt better. When she never got better, she was taken to BSA, a hospital in Amarillo. She died in that hospital three days later, on June 14.

I chose to write my paper about Sarah because even when she was alive, I wanted to be like her. I admire the courage she had to always do what she wanted, even if that meant getting in trouble. As I remember all the great times we had, I can't think of anybody else I would rather call my hero. Sarah was a very special person who loved me more than anyone else, and was always there for me. She touched many people's lives and accomplished many things during her lifetime. Sarah Campbell was not only a great sister, but my best friend and hero."

When Dustin graduated in the spring of 2001 he was trying to get his life back together. A month after graduation he attended a Christian youth retreat and recommitted his life to Christ.

We moved Dustin to Lubbock where he and his best

friend Garland Buske fixed up a little house to live in. While working and remodeling the house, he attended summer school at Texas Tech University. He was adjusting well to college life and living away from home. That fall he moved into the dorm. Dustin and his new roommate Seth Alford became instant friends.

That same year, in August 2001, Stephen started 7th grade and began playing football. A highlight of his year came when Dustin and Seth drove to Tulia to watch his first junior high football game. Dustin promised his little brother he would attend all his games and that thrilled Stephen. Even though they were five years apart in age Dustin and Stephen were close. Stephen missed his sister very much, but Dustin tried to fill the void and doubled his efforts at being both big brother and hero.

Dustin's Friona Chieftain football and baseball pictures.

Stephen's Friona Chieftain football and baseball pictures.
The coaches assigned him Dustin's #77 football jersey.

Chapter 5
Wish You Were Here

Fourteen months had passed since Sarah's death. I bought a real estate business and was working hard to get it established. I had always worked for my husband at Campbell Electric but now I needed something different, something of my own. God provided the opportunity for me to purchase a business, Property Associates Realtors, which I still own today.

One early September day while driving to the bank I turned on the radio and heard a beautiful, yet unfamiliar song. It was about eternal life and how believers who have died are still alive with the Lord. Instead of going to the bank I drove home, called the radio station, and asked for the name of the song. It was "Wish You Were Here," sung by an area musician, Ray Perryman. I felt that through the timing and the words of the song Sarah was telling me how beautiful Heaven is and how she wished we were together. For the next three weeks, each time I thought about the song, I tried to phone Ray Perryman but no one ever answered.

On September 11, 2001, tragedy struck our nation. Dustin called me from Lubbock that morning and then later emailed me. I had no way of knowing that this would be one of the last emails I would ever receive from my son.

From: <ducampbe@ttacs.ttu.edu>
Sent: Tuesday, September 11, 2001 11:09 PM
To: Holly Campbell
Subject: EEEE

Hey mom

How are you? Everything here was really weird today. It is a really sad thing, huh. We watched President Bush on tv and it made me kind of sad, cause you could tell that he was really hurt, and didn't really know what to do. I guess we are really lucky to live in a country as strong as here though. It is really weird how something that far away could affect us that much, but people were freaking out, and there were wrecks everywhere and stuff. I am going to try to come home this weekend, but if gas really goes up like it is supposed to, i wont. I really miss home though - it just isn't the same here. I don't have that feeling of security and stuff, you know. Well, mom, i have homework i need to do, so i am going to go. I hope everything is going to be ok. If something did happen, just know that i love all of you, and i would do anything for you. ill see ya this weekend maybe. love ya.

Dustin

Rainbows Through The Storm

Dustin came home the next weekend to attend a funeral for the mother of his friend Landon. Judy Martin had been struggling with cancer and was only 44 years old when she died. After her funeral we all stood around at the cemetery and wondered whose funeral would be next.

Two weeks later on Friday, September 28, 2001, I was working late at my office on end-of-the-month books. Sarah's death had occurred 15 months earlier. That day Dustin and I had talked on the phone several times. He and some friends were traveling to Austin for a football game against the University of Texas, one of Texas Tech's biggest rivals.

That same evening around 7:00 p.m. I tried once again to call Ray Perryman. This time his wife Kim answered. I identified myself and shared my families' loss and told her how much her husband's song had meant to me. She promised she would mail me a music CD the following day. Only the Lord knew how desperately I would need that song within the next few hours. I was about to have my own September 2001 tragedy.

Earlier that day Danny told me how he had shared his faith with another man whose nephew had died years earlier. Danny said he was finally ready for God to use him in whatever way He saw fit.

At 10:17 that evening Dustin and I spoke for the last time. He phoned to say he and his roommate Seth were almost to San Marcos. I told him to be careful, and he told me to quit worrying so much. He said, "I love you Mom and I'll call you when we get there," then hung up. He and Seth were going to spend that night in San Marcos with some of Sarah's friends and then go to Austin the next day for the game.

At 1:15 a.m., Saturday, September 29th, our phone rang and a female voice identified herself as a nurse at the Breckenridge Hospital in Austin. She asked if I was Dustin Campbell's mother. When I said I was, she informed me that my son had been involved in a vehicle accident. He was dead.

After screaming at the lady, telling her that my daughter had just died and she must be wrong, I threw the phone at Danny. I just sat there stunned and in shock. Moments later our Sheriff and friend Randy Geries knocked on our door to give us the news not realizing we already knew. Witnesses later told us that Dustin had not died instantly but in the helicopter while being airlifted to Austin.

He had been thrown from the Jeep we had given him as a graduation present. We were later told by Seth that he had tried to pass a vehicle and swerved to avoid an oncoming car. He hit a guardrail, went airborne, and crashed into a pole.

Once again our lives were totally shattered. We were barely hanging on after the death of our daughter. Now, how could we face losing our oldest son? I wondered if

I could make it, even with God's help. Word spread and within minutes family and friends gathered at our home. Most of them arrived in a state of shock and disbelief. No one knew what to say.

I couldn't believe that I was about to wake up Stephen in the middle of the night and tell him that his big brother was also dead. We wanted to let him sleep, but word spreads fast and as I looked out my living room window and saw people everywhere I knew we had to tell him before he heard all the noises. I just held him as he quietly stared at me, then went back to sleep.

Stephen later told us that when I woke him up and told him Dustin had been in an accident and was gone he thought he was dreaming and refused to wake up. He said he remembered waking up at 5:30 that morning and hearing everyone in our house. At that point he knew it wasn't a dream.

When Dustin went to college he told Stephen he could have his bedroom so Stephen had just moved all his things. He stayed in his room most of the day and didn't want to see anyone. Neither did I.

Unlike Sarah, we did not get to tell Dustin goodbye. Suddenly, more arrangements had to be made: getting our son's body back to Friona, planning another funeral, and attempting to stay sane. I couldn't imagine how it would all be possible, to endure this all over again. One of the hardest

Dustin

You have shown us the joy a smile can bring, the comfort a hug can give, the peace a prayer brings forth. We had other plans for you and nothing we can say or do can take away the pain of losing you. We cry with hope, grieve with hope, believe with hope, and say goodbye with hope. We believe that all God has said is true; so, it is not really goodbye but more like "see you later". Your smile is forever in our hearts.

Love,
mom and Dad

The bookmark handed out at Dustin's funeral.

things I've ever done in my life was to walk into that funeral home and see my son's lifeless body for the first time.

Once again our family and friends took charge and held us up as we planned another funeral. Again, our friend Waide and his family drove to Friona to preach the funeral. Dustin's high school football coach Bob Ferguson spoke, giving a powerful message to the young people. Our funeral director and friend John created another video to present.

Our friends Raymond and Pam Hamilton drove to Shallowater to get the CD from Ray Perryman with the song "Wish You Were Here". His wife Kim, whom I had never met, attended the funeral. Our music director Kevin Wiseman and his wife Carolyn sang this song at the service.

Patsy made another bookmark. This time it was a picture of Dustin which was taken on a family camping trip one month earlier. Like before, the bookmark had a note from his dad.

We made another drive to a college. This time it was to Texas Tech University where we had to sort through Dustin's belongings. He had one drawer that held pictures of Sarah and a memory book I had made for him. There were personal letters, pictures, and cards from his sister. To me that was more evidence of how much Dustin missed his big sister and of the love he had for her.

We received encouraging letters from the staff at Texas Tech and later attended a memorial service held at the university. We received a picture taken on campus with three flags flown at half mast in Dustin's memory: the American, Texas, and Texas Tech flags. That was quite an emotional day for me.

Another chapter in my life was about to begin. I was about to see if my faith was real or had no meaning at all.

Texas Tech University Campus in Lubbock, Texas

Rainbows Through The Storm

Chapter 6
Praying for Rainbows

In June 2000, when Sarah's friends from San Marcos were driving home after her funeral, they called to tell us they had seen several rainbows from Friona to San Marcos. We talked about how special that was to them. A week later I was feeling sorry for myself and told God I could use a rainbow too.

That evening Stephen was playing baseball. Danny was coaching and I was keeping score when suddenly the sky darkened. In an instant the brightest, most beautiful rainbow I have ever seen appeared. We stopped what we were doing and watched as God hung another rainbow just inside the first one.

That rainbow was mine! To this day rainbows are very special to our family. We have had other rainbows miraculously at times when we have needed some assurance and comfort. To me, this is just another reminder that God is still in control.

On the morning of Dustin's funeral I got on my knees and said, "God, I don't know where You are, and I don't understand what's going on." I knew in my heart my children were saved. I had no doubt they would spend eternity with

My friend Kris took this rainbow picture at the
roadside cross in Groom, Texas.

Jesus, but I still had a hard time comprehending the reality of Heaven and eternity. I needed some assurance that Dustin was in Heaven with Christ and with Sarah. I told the Lord I wanted a rainbow as proof. I know we are not supposed to test God but I was desperate and wasn't thinking clearly.

Dustin's funeral was on a beautiful, clear, cloudless October day, hardly the kind in which rainbows appear. More than one thousand people attended. School was dismissed so students could attend. After a long service we rode once again to the cemetery.

We had been at home only a short time when my friend Carolyn Wiseman knocked on our door. She excitedly told us to come outside and look. There in the sky right over our house was a small rainbow! It stayed in place for the next hour and a half.

At that time no one knew of the prayer I had prayed that morning. Once again God gave me the assurance I needed. I know God is real and He does love us even when we test Him.

#77
DUSTIN CAMPBELL
CLASS OF 2001
CLASSMATE AND FRIEND
A HANDSOME
AND CHARMING GUY
WITH MISCHIEF IN HIS
EYES, KINDNESS IN
HIS HEART, LAUGHTER
ON HIS LIPS AND A
SOUL THAT CONTINUES
TO TOUCH LIVES. WE
CELEBRATE AND
REMEMBER HIS LIFE.

This tree was planted at Friona High School in memory of Dustin
by the Class of 2001 at their 10 year reunion.
Inset picture is a granite tribute to be installed in 2014.

Chapter 7
More Rainbows

After Dustin's death so many unanswered questions had flooded my mind about the accident. I needed to know if Dustin was hurting and conscious. I needed to know if he spoke or asked for me. I won't list all the questions that I was making myself sick over because I didn't have the answers.

On Valentine's Day 2002, I received a letter from a lady in San Marcos. She and her husband had been out driving on a little winding road. The same narrow two-lane road we had told Dustin to avoid because of the dangerous curves and deer. They came upon the accident right after it happened and stopped to render aid. She said she found Dustin and held him until the helicopter came. Though he was unconscious she talked to him anyway. She told him she had a son about his age. Since she didn't know his name she called him Buddy. That happened to be the name of Dustin's dog. After I finished reading the letter I immediately phoned her.

The couple also lived on "Sarah" street in San Marcos. We thought that was pretty cool. It was reassuring to me, as his mother, that in the face of death Dustin was never alone. When I couldn't be there for my son another mother stepped in. Were all these things coincidences? Maybe, but I prefer to believe they were from God.

Since then I have asked God to give me occasional assurances of His presence. I have waited and watched and those reassurances have come in many forms: a rainbow at just the right time, the letter from the lady in San Marcos, a card or gift in the mail on a day I especially needed a lift, a phone call from a friend, a certain verse that stands out when I read my Bible, and the arrival of a special poem from Tom Fuller, titled "I Met Her First Among the Stones." I have included it at the end of the book.

Right after Dustin died Stephen's football coaches gave him Dustin's football jersey #77. It became Stephen's number for the remainder of high school. What an honor for him. Dustin didn't get to fulfill the promise he made to Stephen to be at all his football games. I will always be grateful we had coaches who cared enough to be there for him.

One day shortly after Dustin's death I was feeling really down and decided to drive to Clovis, New Mexico. I drove

 the back roads and as I was driving along I noticed the road sign was 77, our football number. I had never realized it before. For each of us God supplies reminders of what we need to get us through difficult situations. The times I've been at my lowest, God

shows up.

Danny & I surprised Stephen on his 16th birthday with a pickup. We asked the salesman to put the license tags on so it would be ready. I was very nervous about Stephen driving and having a vehicle and was trying very hard to trust God to keep him safe.

When we saw the pickup I noticed that the first two numbers on the license tag were 77. I started crying. We took this as assurance that God is going to watch over our son. Some may think this is coincidence, but I choose to believe it's a God thing. These have been more of our rainbows through the storm.

Both Dustin and Stephen wore #77 when they played Chieftain football.
The number was officially retired at the All-Sports Banquet during
Stephen's senior year. The jersey is displayed in the trophy case
at Friona High School.

Chapter 8
The Storm

When Sarah died my whole world changed. I became immersed in Dustin's activities as a high school senior. When I purchased the real estate business he was my biggest supporter. Three months later he died and my world fell apart again. Everything I valued now seemed worthless. The goals I had set after my daughter's death were meaningless. Still, I worked harder than ever because I did not know what else to do.

In the days and weeks following our losses we faced unexpected challenges. Right after each funeral people returned to work and we were left alone. As time passed the cards and phone calls stopped, however the pain didn't.

I haven't lost my spouse, parents, or siblings but I know that pain will be different. I felt the whole world should have gone into mourning over our loss. It seemed as if our community shifted to watching mode, waiting to see if the Campbells would make it. At times we wondered also.

After Sarah died someone told us how high the divorce rate is for couples who lose a child. That didn't help matters. I didn't ask about the statistics when they lose two!

Our marriage did suffer mainly because men and women

are different. We grieve differently and when couples do not see things exactly the same, the easy way out is to withdraw and drift away from each other.

Danny wanted to grieve alone and Stephen, who was 13, seemed to ignore everything. My heart was aching for him but I didn't know how to help. Stephen wanted to be alone also and would often take our dog Spaz and go hunting for hours at a time to grieve in his own way. Our pilot friend Jim Zehner took Stephen flying several times. Stephen enjoyed flying and it gave him something to look forward to.

Danny and I didn't communicate very well because I needed to talk and he didn't want to. I needed security and encouragement. I needed to be held and loved. At times I felt as though he didn't care and wasn't willing to listen. We didn't understand each other's moods so we often held in our hurts and feelings. We did our best.

When Danny needed to get away to grieve he would go fishing while Stephen and I would do the best we could at home. Five days after Dustin died Danny and Robin, a family friend and co-worker, drove 500 miles to a lake. He had to go away to grieve. This caused resentment and definitely wasn't healthy since a major part of the grieving process is being able to express our hurts, feelings, and needs to one another.

I often worked late. Many times I would ride my bike by myself or go to the high school track and walk, anything to stay busy. Looking back it is apparent that Danny and I often failed each other.

Danny likes to fix things. This time he was unable to fix the problems we faced. He was forced to trust God and have faith that Sarah and Dustin were with Him. I was not so confident. I went through the whys and what ifs. At times I missed them so much I could hardly breathe. Danny wrote about those days from his perspective:

One thing I have done to adjust my life to the fact that we won't see Sarah or Dustin again in this lifetime is to try and live day-to-day. I don't concern myself with things that, in the past, used to seem really important. Even after all this time, going to work is sometimes a bother or a distraction. In the past I had always enjoyed working, but now it seems unimportant. Sometimes work demands more than I am willing to give. My thoughts have become more eternal and less confined to what I see and hear. I try to spend every minute possible with Stephen. Sometimes I worry about smothering him or leaving Holly out.

At times, especially right after Dustin died, I felt like I couldn't grieve or mourn. I had to be strong for Holly and Stephen. Months later I would break down. I felt depressed and apathetic towards work and even my duties at church. The prayer I spoke every morning was, "Lord, give me the strength to see this day through. Only today. We will deal with tomorrow in the morning." Tomorrow had no value to me nor did I have the desire to think about it. I just had to concentrate on one day at a time.

We still want Stephen to be the best he can be. We don't want him drinking or making bad grades, or getting bad haircuts, or talking back to us. But if he does it won't be the end of the world. We will still love him. It's a juggling act, trying to do what is best as a parent without overindulging the children God has blessed us with, especially with only one left here with us. If I could give only one piece of advice it would be, "Parents, love your children no matter what!"

The most positive thing that has come from our loss is that it has made me bolder in my witness. It has also opened doors in ministry that we would otherwise not have had. I have become involved in a prison ministry in which I can share my testimony. Most of these men in prison have had great losses in their own lives and this has created a connection through which I can understand and love them. I have seen God working through our loss to break incredibly hard hearts and bring them to a saving knowledge of Jesus Christ.

After the death of two of my children, I am left with so many unanswerable questions. 2 Corinthians 5:7 NIV says, "We live by faith, not by sight." This has become my motto. This allows God to be God, and allows me to deal with tangible things that I understand.

Chapter 9

One Hour at a Time

In the days following our children's deaths, Danny and I wanted to blame someone. Many of us protective parents tend to blame ourselves for our kids' misfortunes. It would be easy to let Satan drive us insane with a sense of guilt.

I caught myself dwelling on all the things we will never have. Danny will never walk his daughter down the aisle. We will never experience the joy of having grandchildren from Sarah or Dustin. I won't have my daughter to do fun things with or to help me when I'm old. I won't have people telling us we look like sisters anymore.

We say to ourselves, "If only…" and "What if…?" In order to survive another day, even one more hour, at times I pretended Sarah was still in college and only away from home. That fantasy grew impossible when I had to imagine it about both of them.

Parting with my children's personal possessions was especially hard. Danny and I took great pains not to build shrines that would tempt us to dwell in the past. We could have easily closed off the kids' rooms vowing never to use them again. Instead, I bought a small shadow box table to keep their senior rings and a few school mementos.

For four years we kept Sarah's car in the barn. I panicked whenever anyone suggested that we sell it. Eventually we did part with it. Giving it up for someone else's use was a more meaningful tribute to Sarah than letting it gather dust in the barn.

It was difficult going through our kids' clothes and deciding which ones to give away and which ones to keep. We gave some of Sarah's and Dustin's clothes to their friends. My friends Leslie, Linda, and Debbie took t-shirts and jeans and made them into quilts. That gesture meant so much. Now our quilts keep our memories alive and our bodies warm.

I wear a chain that Dustin's friend Audra King gave him for a graduation gift. Dustin always wore the chain but it came off during the wreck. The day after the accident, his friend Garland found it at the wreck site and gave it to me. On that chain I now wear the airplane pendant we gave Sarah while she was taking flying lessons. This is a source of comfort to me and I rarely take it off.

I suggested our family get counseling but Danny and Stephen refused to go. Danny felt like a counselor wouldn't help. He wondered what a counselor could possibly say that would be of any consolation. So I went alone. In the first session the young, childless counselor obviously didn't know what to say to a woman who had two children die. I ended up consoling him.

I went to a different counselor but he too seemed clueless. It's hard even for counselors to find words of comfort if they haven't been there themselves. I also went to a couple of different grief seminars which allowed me to talk about my children. One group consisted of nine widows and widowers, and me. Even though I didn't have anything in common with these people, they were also hurting and they enjoyed having me as part of their group.

In Memory of
SARAH D. CAMPBELL
SARAH'S TREE

This tree was planted in memory of Sarah.

Chapter 10
Relationships

In the wake of tragedy friends find themselves in unfamiliar territory. People treated us differently. They avoided bringing up Sarah and Dustin in conversations, as if saying something would make me think of them and feel pain. The truth is we love talking about them. I think of them anyway, and when people bring up their names it reassures me they are not forgotten. I want my children's memory to live forever.

Some friends began treating me like a stranger at a time when I needed friends more than ever. One confessed to me that it was simply easier and more comfortable not being my friend than struggling to find things to say. I told her she didn't have to say anything at all. Just showing you care and being willing to listen is what is important.

I was not very good at being with people. I needed emotional protection so I pulled into a private little shell. I would not let anyone get too close. I felt self-conscious around others, knowing they were feeling sorry for me. I couldn't stand seeing pity in their eyes.

I returned to work almost immediately because I did not want to be home alone, yet at work it was so hard to concentrate. Carrying on conversations about everyday business was difficult. It all seemed petty and unimportant. Even in groups I felt alone and unable to relate to others.

No one understood. I didn't understand myself, so why should they? I felt isolated and wondered if things would ever be normal again, whatever "normal" is. Still, life goes on with or without us. The calendar never stopped and waited for us to be finished with our grieving. I was still a wife and mom, even though at times I felt ready to hand over those roles to someone else.

We must not forget that in the midst of our grief other family members are hurting also and need our attention. These include grandparents, aunts, uncles, and cousins. Sarah and Dustin had cousins their ages: Lissa, Danny Wayne, Shyla, Amber, Cason, and Doug. We must not forget them or the other cousins and relatives. Grandparents grieve silently so they are also easy to overlook. My children's grandparents not only lost grandchildren, but they also saw their own child hurting. Their grieving was extra hard. My parents lived next door to us, but Danny's mother lived out of town and missed her grandchildren. I felt I had to act strong for their sakes. They in turn tried to act strong for me.

I woke up one morning and couldn't shake my depression. Danny asked me this question, "Holly, if you knew you could only have Sarah for 20 years and Dustin for 18 years would you trade them for two children that you could have for a lifetime?" I realized at that point I would choose Sarah and Dustin. I became thankful for the years I had with them. I wouldn't trade that for anything.

I tried to be sensitive to the needs of Stephen. At times he felt left out and alone. I never wanted to look back in time and realize we were so wrapped up in our own grief that we were not there for him. I honestly do not know how I would have survived without him. Stephen definitely gives us a reason to continue.

We have to come to the place where we do not let guilt paralyze us. I'm a Baptist so I feel guilty about almost everything anyway! That sense was multiplied when my kids died.

Like some teenage girls growing up Sarah went through a rebellious phase. Many times we argued over behavior. Often I have felt regret over the ways we treated her.

She was our first child and we wanted her to be perfect. What a mistake! We would argue over her room not being clean and other petty things that weren't important. Parents, choose your battles with your children. The small things in life are not worth fighting over.

We struggled not to blame Sarah's doctors. They did the best they could. We were advised on several occasions that we should sue them. Doctors are not God. Their knowledge is limited. We felt it would not allow us to heal.

By praying for the doctors and their families it has

allowed some healing in our lives, not bitterness. One doctor has called us several times to let us know he is thinking of us. Did they make mistakes, or was it simply God's will for Sarah to die when she did? Or was it both? Does it really matter? If you know the answer, my address will be in the back of this book!

Though we ask ourselves questions like these after tragedy, eventually we must put them behind us unanswered. I will never fully understand why my children died until I get to Heaven. I do have a few questions for God and I think that it will be okay to ask Him.

I have often wondered what my obligation is and how can I truly LET GO and LET GOD work through me? I want to be able to help others who are hurting and grieving. I want to be an example to others showing them that they can make it through life's difficult paths. I want everyone to know that Christ wants to be the center of our lives. Even though we sin every single day, He still loves us.

There is no way I can do any of this on my own strength without Christ being my guide and my helper. Without Him, I am nothing. I have tried doing things on my own and I usually make a mess.

Chapter 11
Forever Changed

We go through several stages of grief: shock, denial, depression, anger, and guilt. I don't know how many stages there are, I never knew which one I was in, and I got frustrated trying to figure it out. Grief is exhausting! I was usually in several stages at the same time. I'm sure the stages were different with each child but I can't remember. I'm pretty sure one stage is memory loss!

If you ever have a child who dies or face some other terrible tragedy, expect to have feelings that you have never experienced before. You will feel guilty. In your memory the disagreements you had will be magnified.

You will feel guilt over the things you should have done or hard words that were exchanged. You may feel like you are suffocating, like you need to escape from your situation, but cannot.

You will feel angry, depressed, and lonely. Your heart will hurt in a way it has never hurt before. At times you will think you are losing your mind. All of these strange and confusing feelings are normal.

One Sunday afternoon I drove to the cemetery with a blanket and a book. I fell asleep beside their graves. The pain and emptiness I felt was almost unbearable. I was overwhelmed and out of control.

I cried out to God and begged Him to ease the pain. I'm not sure how long I stayed there that day. Finally in the background I heard an airplane landing at the airport nearby. I knew that Sarah and Dustin were near, encouraging me, and I felt somewhat at peace.

Accept that life will never again be the same. That is not as terrible as it sounds. Life is full of changes over which we have no control. People who never change, never grow.

Different people have asked me how I handle the pain of my children dying. I tell them I don't have a choice. I either let the pain embitter me or I let it better me. Being bitter is awfully miserable. The question that matters is: Will you grow and get better or end up bitter? Your loss doesn't have to be a death for you to experience such feelings. Friends have told me the "empty nest" is lonely and depressing too.

Your loss will be easier to accept if you surrender to Jesus Christ. Because I am a Christian I believe earthly life is temporary. I choose to believe my children are on a wonderful vacation in a special place called Heaven. I like to picture Sarah welcoming Dustin when he died. Someday we will see them again and join them for all Eternity. That makes death easier to bear.

You can expect emotional setbacks on all your firsts: their birthdays, Mother's Day, Thanksgiving and Christmas, the anniversaries of their deaths, their friends getting married and having babies, college graduations, and more.

In spite of our Christian beliefs we still experience difficult days. I feel I have no control over anything. No matter how hard I pray or focus on positive thoughts I cannot bring my children back. In my helplessness I am forced to look to God for strength and guidance to survive each day.

Some days I miss Dustin more than Sarah, and other days it's the opposite. At both times I feel guilty as if I loved one more than the other.

EASTERN NEW MEXICO
FLIGHT ACADEMY
PO BOX 1962 * CLOVIS, NM 88102-1962 * 505 389 1224*email:enmfa@etsc.net

NEWSLETTER NUMBER 147   JULY 2000

High Flight

By John Gillespie Magee Jr.

Oh, I have slipped the surly bonds of Earth
And danced the skies on laughter-silvered wings;
Sunward I've climbed,
And joined the tumbling mirth of sun-split clouds
And done a hundred things you have not dreamed of
Wheeled and soared and swung
High in the sunlit silence
Hovering there,
I've chased the shouting wind along,
And flung my eager craft through footless halls of air.
Up, up the long, delirious, burning blue
I've topped the windswept heights with easy grace
Where never lark, or even eagle flew.
And, while with silent, lifting mind I've trod
The high untrespassed sanctity of space,
Put out my hand, and touched the face of God.

Sarah

We are saddened to learn that Sarah Campbell joined those that have made their last flight. You might remember that Sarah was our teen age aviatrix with the bubbly personality. She earned her Private Certificate two days before she departed for college in 1998.

Sarah has joined the other avid aviators of Eastern New Mexico Flight Academy that have also had their last flight.

1988-2000
We Remember and Honor

Jim Guest	Grant Hudson	Stephen Norris	Chad Pharies
	Grover Poole	Clyde Reynolds	John Riddle

Newsletter from Eastern New Mexico Flight Academy
honoring Sarah.

Chapter 12
Pennies from Heaven

Days turn into weeks, months, and years. The grief process may change but it is always there in some form. As the days passed for me I began to look for simple ways to deal with those daily thoughts. As silly as it may seem, the little games I play provide some relief by lifting my spirits and keeping Sarah's and Dustin's memories alive in my heart.

The post office is a popular place in our small town. Each day I go to my post office box to get the mail. There used to be a stamp machine for people to buy stamps when the post office was closed. The change used to buy them was not an exact amount so an extra 3 cent stamp would be returned by the machine. Many people left the 3 cent stamp. When I saw the extra stamps I pretended they were Sarah and Dustin blowing me a kiss and I took and pasted them on a blank piece of paper at my office. Unfortunately the post office no longer offers this service.

My friend Kayla gave me a poem entitled "A Penny." It was about angels and pennies and meant a lot to me. So now when I see a penny on the ground I pretend it is from Sarah if it is heads up and Dustin if it is tails up. It makes me smile when I find one.

These are some of the silly things I do but I have come to realize that in our grief it is okay to be silly. It makes me smile, it brightens my day, and it makes me feel a little closer to them.

Here is the "penny poem" my friend gave me. I hope you enjoy it. I keep it framed near my desk and it gives me comfort.

"A Penny"

I found a penny today
Just lying on the ground.
But it's not just a penny
This little coin I've found.

Found pennies come from Heaven
That's what a dear friend told me.
She said angels toss them down
Oh, how I love to hear that story.

She said when an angel misses you
They toss a penny down.
Sometimes just to cheer you up
When you are feeling down.

So, don't pass by that penny
If you feel there's no one who cares
It may be a penny from Heaven
From your angels, Sarah and Dustin.

Chapter 13
Journey Back

When you have a child die you are never the same again. Suddenly nothing in life matters. Recovery becomes a lifelong journey. Your values and opinions will be different on almost everything.

Since people are not accustomed to dealing with death they say and do strange things. Some will rush to your side to help you, but once they arrive they actually add to your injury. Others abandon you altogether. Most do not mean harm, but it hurts just the same.

About six months after Dustin's death we traveled to the scene of his wreck. I had to see the place where my son died. His friends had made a cross and placed it at the site next to the road, and we set out new flowers. After we returned home I told an acquaintance where we had been and she responded, "You mean you're not over that yet?"

When Sarah died, another friend said, "I know exactly how you feel. My grandmother died ten years ago." No, losing a grandmother is not the same. You can't know how it feels until you go through it. No one but me knows how I feel. I don't know how Danny or Stephen feel. At times I don't even know how I feel. It's also very hard for me to listen to my friends complain about their children. Sometimes I feel that others have forgotten about my kids. I try really hard to understand that people don't mean to be insensitive.

After Dustin died we felt like we had to be strong for everyone else. If we didn't smile and show confidence it implied we were not good Christians. Actually we needed to be allowed to be weak.

When loved ones die we need to talk about it. We need to talk about them. No deep theological answers are expected. Talking helps. We need friends and family who allow us to express our true thoughts, doubts, and feelings without condemning us.

We don't need Christian clichés like, "He's in a better place" and "God picked the prettiest flower in the garden for His own." While those thoughts may seem comforting, they raise all kinds of issues. Never tell people whose children have died that their kids are better off or it's time to get on with life. Those comments cut like a knife! We need someone to hold us, someone quiet and kind who will let us express anything we feel without judging us.

Sacrificial acts of kindness help also. After Sarah died, for several weeks my friend Leslie came to our home, gathered up the laundry, washed it, and brought it back to us. Others continued bringing food and sending cards. My aunt Lois traveled from Arizona and stayed several extra days to help my mom, sisters, and me write the many thank-yous.

Let people grieve in whatever ways they must without judging them. God made us each unique and no one should look down on anyone else for grieving differently. Now when I attempt to comfort someone who has had a loved one die, I offer a hug and prayer and tell them I'm willing to listen. It's showing you care that's important.

To help deal with my grief I like to sit at the cemetery. I used to think our cemetery was creepy but now I find it peaceful. Many times I have gone there and found letters or items from different friends. My kids have pretty headstones with colored rainbows carved into them.

So when my day gets too crazy I go hide for awhile with my kids, even though I know they aren't really there. To me it's quiet and serene and I can talk to them and to God. The Friona airport is nearby so I can often watch the airplanes come and go.

The best way I deal with my grief is to stay busy. Danny and Stephen like to go fishing and hunting. Because they both enjoy the same things they spend a lot of time together. I knew that I needed something fun in my life besides working all the time.

One year for my birthday Danny gave me ten paid piano lessons. That was one of the best gifts I have ever received. Now when I'm home alone I enjoy playing the piano.

I also found some of Sarah's beginner flute music and

enjoy playing her flute. I almost sold it after she died and now I am so thankful that my friend Alan talked me out of it.

I bought a fancy digital camera and love photography. Ron Carr, the owner and editor of our local newspaper, encouraged me to learn more about photography. He has helped me with my new camera. This is a fun hobby and Ron even uses some of my photos in the newspaper and gives me credit just to make me feel special.

My mom and I work at the newspaper office every Thursday morning labeling newspapers and taking them to the post office. We have done this since I was a little girl and now I tell people this is my "fun" job. We have all become friends working a few hours a week together. They have loved and supported me through fun and sad times.

I became especially close to Marlene Mueller who worked at the Friona Star. Her son Monty was killed in a vehicle accident in 1988 when he was 19, so she understood my pain and was always willing to listen when I needed to talk. We have a special bond because of our children. She has helped me to realize that life does go on.

We had a scholarship fund at our local bank and each year at graduation we would honor a graduating senior in memory of Sarah. This was one way we could help someone else and keep her memory alive.

In a final bit of irony, we established the scholarship in memory of Sarah, and Dustin was the first recipient. He only had one month of college before he died. Then we had a scholarship in memory of both Sarah and Dustin. In May 2005, we presented the scholarship to a family member, Jeremy Campbell. The scholarship ended in 2007 when Stephen graduated and was the last recipient.

Danny, Stephen and Shadow at Ute Lake in Logan, New Mexico.
Fishing is their favorite pastime.

Chapter 14
Out of Our Control

A question I will always struggle with is: Why did my children die? Regardless of the reason I know that God has used Sarah's and Dustin's deaths for His purposes. Many people have come to the saving knowledge of Christ as a result of their deaths. I must believe my children did not die in vain and that God does create good out of tragedy.

On Dustin's death certificate it was noted that alcohol was a factor. That check mark was like a blow to my heart, something I was not prepared to see. Alcohol was found in his jeep. I never thought my child would drink and drive. I felt we had instilled that value in our children. I had talked to him less than an hour before his wreck and he sounded fine to me.

I didn't know whether to be angry with Dustin or believe his friends who told us that he was not drinking. I can't ask Dustin so I have to tell every teenager and adult the danger of drinking and driving. I have to accept the fact that I'll never know for sure what happened that night in Dustin's jeep and why he made the decision he did.

Another nagging question is: Did I let my kids down because I failed to protect them?

After Sarah died Danny and I bought Dustin a bright yellow Jeep Wrangler for his high school graduation. Tragically, he was driving it when he died. Of course we wondered if we were at fault.

I have to try hard not to be overly protective of our surviving child. On Stephen's 15th birthday we bought two new four-wheelers. Two days later Stephen and I spent a couple of hours riding around in the country and having fun.

On the way home Stephen decided to ride in the pasture beside the dirt road. He was speeding along the bumpy ground when suddenly I watched in horror as he hit a hidden ditch, flew through the air, and he and the four-wheeler tumbled and flipped repeatedly. Later he told me the only thing he could hear was his mom screaming hysterically. I drove up to him not knowing if he were alive or dead.

He was lying very still and told me that everything hurt. I felt sure his neck was broken. I used his cell phone to call my brother and I was so hysterical I couldn't tell him where we were. Stephen had to talk to him on the phone to give directions.

The ambulance, fire truck, and police officers finally found us. After x-rays and tests at the hospital, the doctor told us the only thing broken was his collarbone. We truly gave God the credit for taking care of him; however, his football coaches were not too happy since they had plans to use him in the starting line-up on the junior varsity football team.

Later I had to deal with comments of well-meaning friends asking me things like, "What were you thinking?" or "I can't believe you bought Stephen a four-wheeler after your other two kids died!" I was already beating myself up and didn't need their contributions. We need to let our kids have fun and take risks, but how do we know what to do and where to draw the line? Once again a sense of guilt overwhelmed me.

We have to realize that there are things in life beyond our control. Should we force our children to live in a bubble, or let them experience life and trust in our Heavenly Father? I know that God is always in control, but He does allow us to make choices. When we make the wrong choices we suffer the consequences.

When I was first writing this book, Stephen celebrated his 16th birthday. We have to trust God for his safety and protection.

Holly's Real Estate office located on Highway 60 in Friona.

After Stephen graduated from college he returned to Friona and
joined his dad in our Campbell Electric business.

Chapter 15
After the Storm

Danny, Stephen, and I made a decision that we will not turn away from God no matter how difficult life is. "Fake it till you make it" became my motto. At times I have to act happy while inside my heart is breaking.

When bad things happen our human nature wants to blame someone or something. It becomes easy to fault or condemn God. After all, He could have healed Sarah and prevented Dustin's accident. But for reasons only He knows, He chose not to. It's okay to ask "Why?" and yes, I did blame God and I still wonder why my children died. We don't have to understand everything to trust Him. I can't change the whys or the what ifs. If I dwell on the what ifs they will destroy me.

At a church gathering a friend told how God had spared his son in a vehicle accident. Why does God let some be spared but not others? I don't know and I don't pretend to know. I won't ever have all my questions answered on this earth. That doesn't mean there are no answers. We don't understand the stars but that doesn't mean they're not there.

My role is to focus on God's will for my life and use my tragedy to help others. In 2 Corinthians 12:9 NIV, Paul writes that the Lord said, "My grace is sufficient for you, for my power is made perfect in weakness." I'm glad it is, for at times I have felt awfully weak!

We need to trust our Heavenly Father no matter what. Sometimes our will is not God's will and our ways are not His ways. See Isaiah 55:8 NIV. If we choose to trust God anyway, He will help us through. God is faithful and loves each and every one of us.

We know the Bible verses that say, "Ask and it will be given to you" Matthew 7:7 NIV, and "For where two or three come together in my name, there am I with them" Matthew 18:20 NIV. It would be easy to jump to conclusions and twist the meaning: "If God really loves us He will do what we say, every time." But that's not what they mean.

I had to decide to put my complete faith and trust in God, or to turn away from Him and grow bitter. I had to choose to believe God's promises or to reject them. I do have faith that my children are spending eternity with Christ, and I want to see them again; therefore, I choose God and His promises. I also had to choose deliberately that I would not let Satan destroy me with doubts, though occasionally he still tries.

My thinking still gets confused. I know my children are better off in Heaven, but I still want them here with me. I'm their mom and I miss them and need them. There are things I want to talk to them about. I want to hear their voices. At these times I'm confused, God isn't. His thinking is perfect and clear (all-knowing) and I have to trust His wisdom because it is higher than mine.

Even if you have never lost anyone to death you may carry some kind of hurt in your heart, whether it's divorce, abuse, rejection, addiction, etc. Sometimes life simply isn't fair. God never promised us it would be, but He does promise that He will be with us through the unfairness and heartaches of life if we put our trust and faith in Him.

Have you ever heard the saying, "God won't give you more than you can handle"? People have quoted that to me and I began looking for it in the Bible. I can't find it anywhere, but I do believe that when life gives us more than we can handle God carries us through the storm.

Because my family decided to trust God completely, even during times when we didn't understand Him, we are now able to look back and see all the places the Lord was present during our ordeals. Many times during our grieving we were not even aware of His loving hand. Nevertheless, He was always there behind the scenes perfectly orchestrating the events in our lives.

Sarah had gone through a rebellious phase. She tried smoking, drinking, and even drugs. Many times we were at odds, but the night before her surgery we were walking through the streets of San Marcos admiring the old Victorian homes. Suddenly she stopped and said, "Thank you Mom for never lowering your standards for me and never giving up on me." Hearing that was wonderful, and has truly been a comfort to me.

Several days later at the hospital the last words Sarah ever said to me before she died were "Mom, don't be a dork!" It was a simple statement that showed her personality and is one of the memories that makes me smile.

Chapter 16
Promises

2 Corinthians 5:7 NIV tells us, "We live by faith, not by sight." Our story seems to be one of tragedy, death, and defeat. It could end that way but I choose to look at it from the viewpoint of eternity. After experiencing these trials, I am not afraid to die. I have already realized my worst fear twice. Death has no hold on us or our children. That battle was won on the cross by Jesus Christ.

Romans 8:38-39 says, "For I am persuaded, that neither death, nor life, nor angels, nor principalities, nor powers, nor things present, nor things to come, nor height, nor depth, nor any other creature, shall be able to separate us from the love of God, which is in Christ Jesus our Lord." If the death of two of our children has not been able to separate us from Jesus, we know nothing will.

Parents, pray for your children and make sure they belong to Christ. It's the most important thing you can do for them. Make that a top priority in your life. In the end nothing else really matters. God desires each of us to have a personal relationship with Jesus. He wants our love and our obedience more than anything else.

Mark 12:30 NIV says, "Love the Lord your God with

all your heart and with all your soul and with all your mind and with all your strength." God desires us to read the Bible and seek Him. He longs for us to talk to Him, then He tells us to be still and listen. God has given me the grace I've needed to survive. Many times it's been a day or an hour or a minute at a time. Without Him I wouldn't be here today sharing my story.

How do I pray? 1 Thessalonians 5:18 says "In everything give thanks." Ephesians 5:20 tells us that we should be "Giving thanks always for all things." That's pretty simple and clear, yet very hard for me to do after the deaths of two children. Is it even realistic to try? Yes, it is.

Chapter 17
Hope and Faith

I am thankful for memories that can never be taken away. In my prayers I thank God and tell Him how I'm feeling. I ask Him to comfort and take care of us. I am thankful that, even though the death of a child is not good, in all things God is working for good.

Sometimes I feel empty and don't know how to pray. When that happens I tell God, "Here I am. Hold me and take care of me. I'm doing the best I can." He knows our hearts anyway so we might as well be honest.

Because of our tragedies other people have come to Christ. At Dustin's funeral a close friend of mine accepted Christ as her Lord and Savior. Soon both of her children did too, and we were present when they were baptized.

Danny shares our story in prisons. I received a letter from a young convict who wrote to tell me how many prisoners accepted Christ as a response. I pray that nothing we have endured will be wasted, that in all things, even this, "God works for the good of those who love Him, who have been called according to His purpose" Romans 8:28 NIV.

I do have hope. I have faith that God loves you and me unconditionally. He offers each of us eternity with Him. We have to choose whether to accept or reject Him. Hebrews 11:1 NIV says, "Now faith is being sure of what we hope for and certain of what we do not see."

Hope and faith go together. I hold hope that there is a Heaven and that I will see Sarah and Dustin there, for all of eternity. Having faith is casting doubts aside and believing with certainty in this hope. Faith is trusting Jesus Christ to deliver me from my sins. Even though I cannot see Heaven, and I can't prove its existence, God has instilled in me the faith to believe.

If you don't have Christ in your heart I am asking you to accept Him right now. We are not guaranteed tomorrow, not even one more minute. If you need to talk to your spouse, children, parents, friends, or anyone else to seek forgiveness, do it today. In my heart I know we will spend eternity with Sarah and Dustin in the presence of our Lord. Don't pass up this opportunity to be there with us.

"For God so loved the world, that he gave his only begotten Son, that whosoever believeth in him should not perish, but have everlasting life." John 3:16

Conclusion
By Danny

So, where does this leave us? After the death of a child it leaves us asking where God is. Does He answer prayer?. Does praying do any good? In our case, the answer to both questions is yes.

On several occasions God has answered my prayers. Sometimes it has been yes. Sometimes it has been no. Once He simply said "Trust Me". He loves me so much that He sent His Son to die in my place. He loves Sarah and Dustin just as much. I can't help but trust someone who loves me like that.

If we believe God's word is undeniably and completely true, then we must conclude that He does answer prayer. The problem is that we live in a fallen, imperfect world. When God does heal it only extends life on this earth temporarily. I don't pretend to know why He sometimes says "No" or "Trust Me". His reasons are beyond my understanding.

When tragedy and pain come your way the only thing I truly know to tell you is to crawl up in God's lap and let Him love and comfort you.

We are still learning from our children. Sarah taught us never to judge anyone and to accept people for who they are. Dustin taught us that it's okay to laugh and have fun. We are still learning from Stephen. He has taught us that attitude is everything. Thank you Sarah, Dustin, and Stephen. You have each taught us SO much.

In Memory of Sarah Campbell
1979-2000

In Memory of Dustin Campbell
1983-2001

We donated this bench to the new Friona hospital in memory
of Sarah and Dustin. Holly is with her parents, Laura and Dale Hart.

Epilogue

I completed writing this book five years after Sarah died. Writing has been therapy for me. It has brought about some healing. However, I will miss my children every day for the rest of my life. Some days are easier than others. I am so thankful for our son Stephen and other family members and friends who have encouraged and prayed for us. In 2013, I revised and updated the book and added a few more pictures.

Danny continues to work for himself as an electrician and still fishes as often as possible. He was offered a job teaching woodworking at Friona High School and taught from 2007 until 2011. He chose to stop when Stephen graduated from college so they could work together. Before he accepted the teaching job, Danny was involved in a prison ministry which was very healing for him.

Stephen graduated from Friona High School in 2007, and graduated from Tarleton State University in Stephenville, Texas in May 2011. He bought a house in Friona in 2012 and moved back to help his dad in the family business, Campbell Electric. Stephen is also a member of the Friona Volunteer Fire Department and has plans to attend the Fire Academy.

When Stephen was a senior at Friona High School, the school administration retired the number 77 from the football program. Both Dustin and Stephen wore this number and one of their jerseys now hangs in the trophy case at our high school gym. What an honor! Stephen is an amazing young man and definitely gives us joy and a reason to stay positive.

I continue to sell and manage property through my real estate business. I also own a fitness center and continue to do bookkeeping for Danny and Stephen at Campbell Electric. I am grateful to God for my success and for having a vocation that keeps me busy.

Danny and I speak at high schools, churches, and other groups about choices and decisions. This has brought some healing in our lives.

I had the honor one summer to be part of a very special young lady's wedding. Katy Baize, a family friend, lost her mother tragically when she was nine years old. Now grown, she asked me to stand in and be her "mom" for her special wedding day. Thank you Katy. I love you.

Today things are as normal as can be expected at the Campbell house. Our faith and our memories sustain us through each and every day, one day at a time. We have indeed found rainbows through the storm.

Danny, Holly, & Stephen Campbell
P.O. Box 471
Friona, TX 79035
email: hollyrcampbell@hotmail.com

Stephen, Holly, Danny, and Shadow.

The Serenity Prayer

God grant me the

serenity to accept

the things I

cannot change,

the courage to

change the things

I can, and the

wisdom to know

the difference.

One day at a time...

Acknowledgements

This book was written to help me work through my grief. I began keeping a journal after Sarah died and have continued to do so. As I go back and re-read it I am able to see that God was there even when I didn't realize it. He was there through every heartache and pain, through every tear. I wouldn't be where I am today without Him being right here beside me. Thank you Lord.

To Danny and Stephen: a wonderful husband and son. You have encouraged me to continue writing when I wanted to quit. You have been patient and understanding and have helped me with the wording of this book. Thank you both for being a part of this adventure and for your many prayers.

To all of Sarah's and Dustin's friends who have continued to stay a part of our lives. You have helped so much by sharing funny and memorable stories of Sarah and Dustin and have continued to love our family. You have each found ways to make sure they will not be forgotten. Thank you for sharing your lives with us.

A very special thank you to Dr. Tom Fuller who encouraged me to write this book. Thank you for helping me and for being there to share my pain. When I met you that day in the Friona cemetery I added another friend. You were the one who encouraged me to speak and write about our children's death and to keep going and stay positive.

My friend Kayla McLennan for encouraging me to tell my family's story. She covered for me many times at work when I couldn't be there. Our friendship began as soon as I met Kayla. Her family planted a tree in their front yard in Sarah's memory on the one year anniversary of her being in Heaven, even though they never knew Sarah. Every time I drive by the house I see our "Sarah" tree. What an honor. I will always cherish our friendship.

A very special thank you to Ron Carr, Cynthia Smith, and Scott Haffner for editing and proofing my book. They have offered positive suggestions that have helped me so much. Thank you for your friendship and for all your many hours of help.

Nathan Parson designed the front and back cover, scanned pictures, and was always willing to help with anything I needed on the computer. Thank you for your time and patience.

To Clint Mears at Intheden Graphics for helping me with the final preparation to get my book to the printer.

And to all my family and friends who never gave up on me and have continued to encourage and pray for Danny, Stephen, and me. You are all a special part of my life.

I Met Her First Among the Stones

Tom Fuller

I met her first among the stones,
   A cemetery, dead and dry.
She did not blend, amid those bones,
   Beneath that gray, depressing sky.

The entourage, as always, fared
   As e'er they manage at these things –
The bent, the slow and snowy-haired,
   Their every effort made with pains.

Contrasting, she seemed out of place,
   Was younger, almost as a child,
With darker hair and comely face;
   As others wept, she faintly smiled.

What kind of mourner could she be,
   Who stood before me, here, and now?
With all the grief around, did she
   Not fully comprehend, somehow?

However, she, incongruous,
   Smiled pleasantly, above the moans,
Apart, almost oblivious,
   Mid sighing friends and silent stones.

Then, when the service came to close,
    She finally said a word to me,
And I, a counselor who knows,
    Observed what others could not see.

Her smile, it covered something more:
    A deeper hurt, a private pain
That she and no one else there bore;
    A burden covered o'er in vain.

She introduced herself to me,
    And thanked me for the thoughtful word,
My recent spoken eulogy,
    The message which she'd lately heard.

And after proper time passed by –
    With clear control, and no laments –
She started then to tell me why
    She stood among these monuments:

The boy o'er whom I'd said the prayer,
    Whose life, too soon, had met its end,
This young man, tall and dark and fair,
    A family friend of hers had been.

He'd known her girl and older son,
    The lot of them had all been friends.
Together they had had their fun,
    Had waged their wars, and made amends.

I wondered how this mother who
   Had known the younger man for years,
Could, at the same time talk this through
   In calm control, and shed no tears.

I asked her how her kids had fared,
   Considering their friend's demise.
She told me they had not despaired,
   Nor bidden any sad goodbyes.

Then asked she if I'd like to meet
   Her children, for they, too, were near.
I answered I would love to greet
   Her kids. I had not seen them here.

She turned and walked, not toward the place
   Where people still were standing 'round,
But off into a distance space,
   Across the sad and stony ground.

We ambled o'er the grassy clay.
   I knew not why; I dared not ask;
But not a sentence did we say,
   And not a word between us passed.

We finally reached our journey's end,
   A lonely corner of the park.
I saw the lady's gaze suspend
   On two small granites, newly marked.

We stood, with still no word exchange,
　　And then it was, I grew aware:
Carved on the stones I saw the names
　　of "Sarah" here, and "Dustin" there.

Her only daughter first was taken,
　　An illness snatched her from her sight.
And then, this mother, yet forsaken,
　　Gave up her son one violent night,

T'was in a terrible collision,
　　The kind that every parent fears:
A driver's sudden indecision,
　　That took him, only eighteen years.

I searched for words to say that would
　　Bring comfort, but I sought in vain.
No, nothing came, for nothing could
　　Make lighter her enormous pain.

Then I began to realize
　　No aid was needed there from me,
For she saw One with inner eyes –
　　A Helper Whom I could not see,

A Shepherd in a Higher Sphere,
　　Pursued and tended her at length,
A Friend Who, unlike any here,
　　Conversed with her, and gave her strength.

When families are torn asunder,
  It haunts the heart and sears the soul;
But through the storm, we're sheltered under
  The wings of One who can console

The deepest grief, the tortured thought,
  The dark returning after night;
He takes the sightless, overwrought,
  And, in His time, provides His light.

The burden parents cannot bear,
  Which they, alone, could ne'er abide,
He, kindly, and will gently share,
  Until they find the Other Side.

One time I gave a eulogy,
  With lofty talk and lucid word;
But her silent sermon preached to me
  Was better than I've ever heard.

And someday, when it's time for me
  The dreaded race of death to run,
Her face, and Friend, I hope to see,
  And her smile assure, "It can be done."

(Composed on Sarah's 24th Birthday)

Special Acknowledgements

On Easter Sunday 2000, Danny, Dustin, Stephen, and I went to San Marcos to see Sarah. Before going to church that Easter morning I took a picture of them standing in front of Sarah's fireplace in her apartment.

After Dustin died, my dad took this picture to our friend and artist Carol Ellis. He asked Carol to paint a picture of Sarah and Dustin standing on a golden road with a rainbow over their heads and a cross in the background. The painting was a gift for me. Thank you Daddy.

The front cover is a picture of the painting. If you look closely you can see an angel to the left of Sarah's head. Thank you Carol. I will treasure my painting always.

About the Artist

Carol Ellis first picked up a paintbrush at age 13 and has been in love with art ever since. Carol says she paints "memories from the heartbeat of a simpler time." Her subjects range from western landscapes, ranchlands, and farmyard scenes to Victorian flower gardens and oil portraits.

This award-winning journalist and ribbon-winning artist paints almost exclusively in oils, showing a true flair for color and design. "I like the permanency of oil painting, and the feeling that I am leaving something of myself for others to enjoy for years to come," states Mrs. Ellis. She studied commercial art at OCW but ended up with a journalism degree from Texas Tech.

Carol and her husband Bill are longtime residents of Friona, Texas. They published the *Friona Star* newspaper from 1962 until 2003. They also published an academic and athletic history of Friona ISD, *Friona On Parade*, in 2006. It chronicles school events from 1908 until 2005.

This is the photo Carol Ellis used for the rainbow painting
of Sarah and Dustin.

Notes

Notes

Notes